Find and circle the following object... Pilgrim village: ear of corn, fish, hat, turkey, to..., spoon, cornucopia, pie, frying pan, candy corn.

# Help the Pilgrim find his way through the ship to the food.

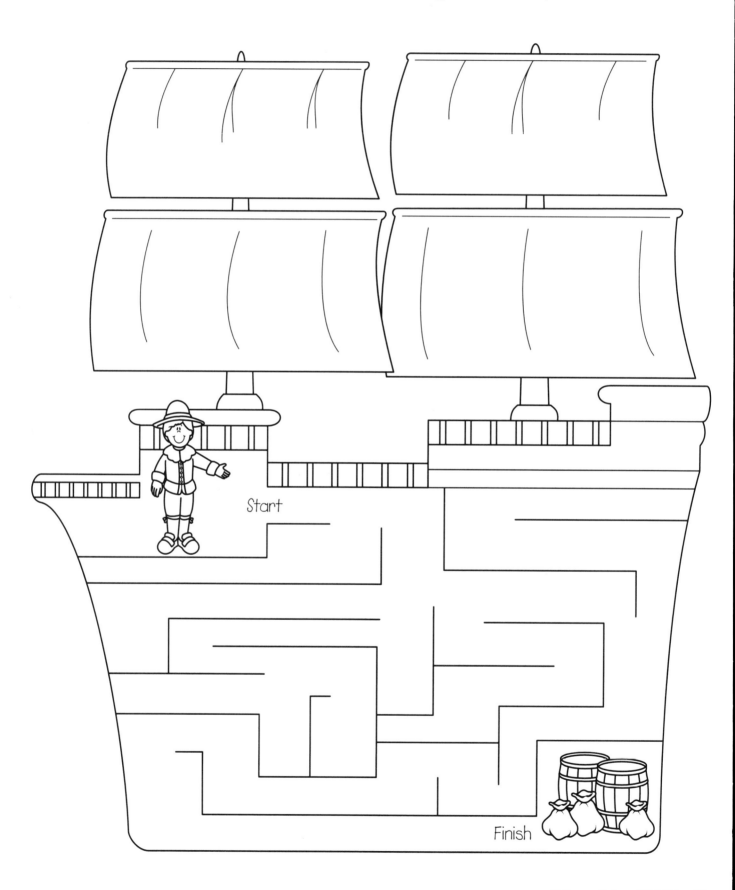

Start

Finish

Color the cornucopia.

# Complete the crossword puzzle with Thanksgiving words.

## Across

1. The _____ sailed to the New World.
2. We give _____ for food.
5. Pilgrims traveled in this ship.
7. You do this when you're hungry.
8. An adult will _____ the turkey with a knife.
9. Sit at the _____ to eat.

## Down

1. The Pilgrims landed at _____ Rock.
3. Farmers _____ their crops in the fall.
4. A word meaning "to collect" or "to get together as a group" is _____.
6. A large holiday dinner may be called a _____.

Cut out the puzzle pieces and paste them on another
sheet of paper to form a picture. Color the picture.

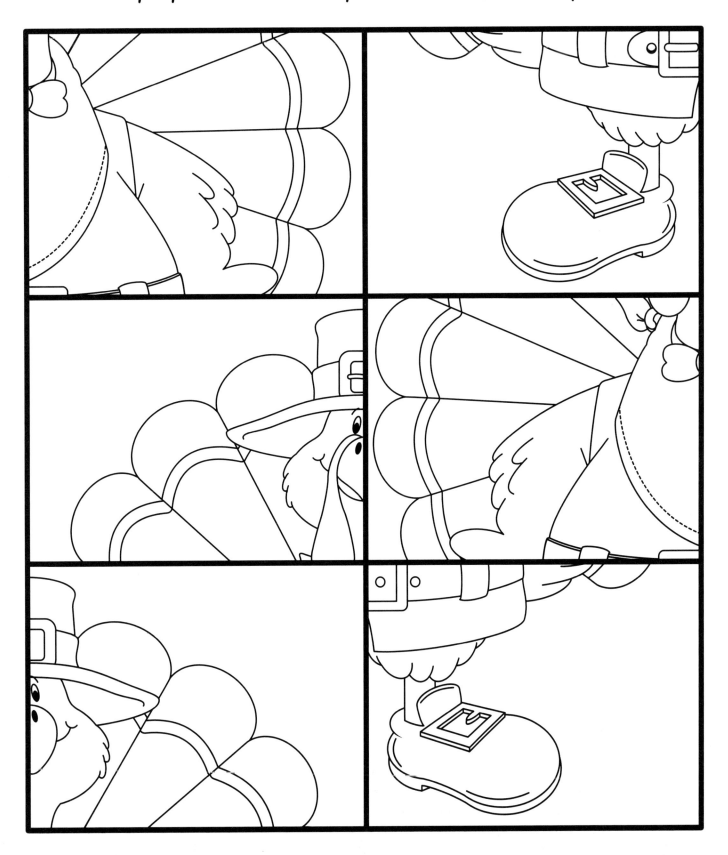

Find and circle the Thanksgiving words from the word list below.

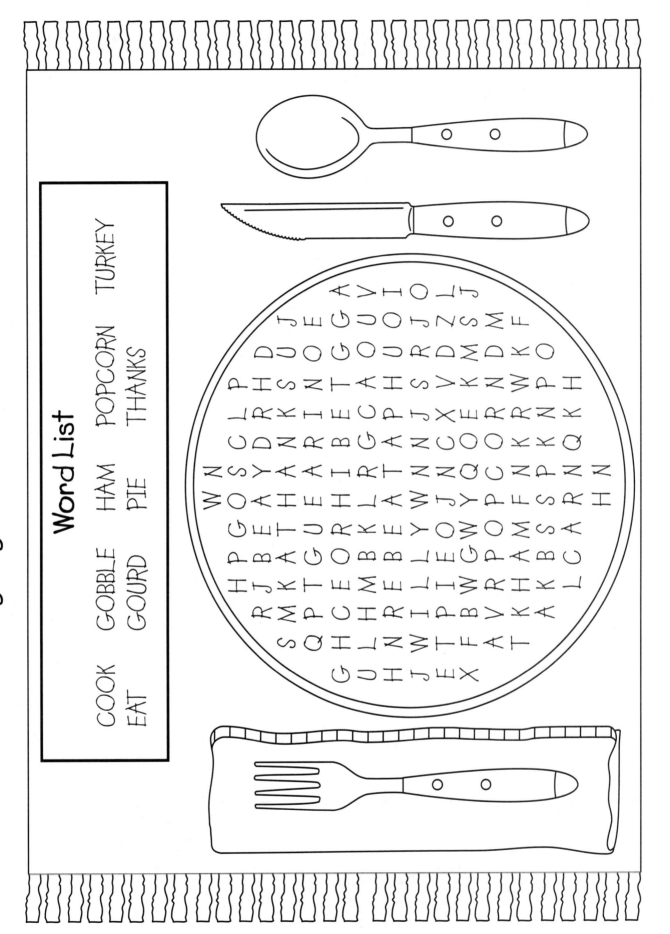

Word List

COOK      GOBBLE    HAM    POPCORN    TURKEY
EAT       GOURD     PIE    THANKS

# Unscramble the Thanksgiving foods to answer the riddle.

1. TTEOPOAS     (P) O T A T O E S
2. PPALES       _ _ _ _ _ _
3. MYSA         _ _ _ _
4. EAZMI        _ _ _ _ _
5. CORANBERD    _ _ _ _ _ _ _ _
6. KUPPNIM IPE  _ _ _ _ _ _ _   _ _ _
7. FFUSTING     _ _ _ _ _ _ _ _
8. QUSSAH       _ _ _ _ _ _
9. AVYRG        _ _ _ _ _
10. IONNOS      _ _ _ _ _ _
11. BRANERRIESC _ _ _ _ _ _ _ _ _ _ _
12. YRUTKE      _ _ _ _ _ _

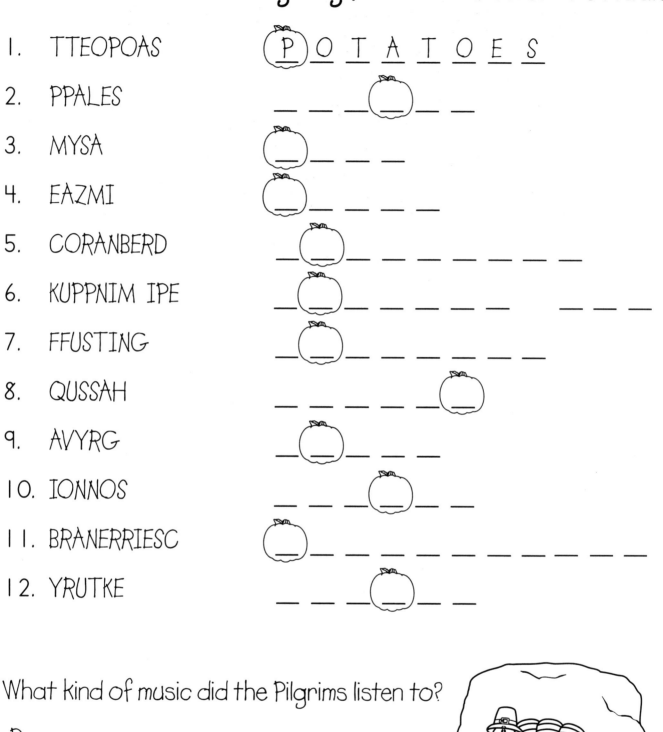

What kind of music did the Pilgrims listen to?

P _ _ _ _ _ _ _   _ _ _ _

Connect the dots to see what food Native Americans taught the Pilgrims how to grow. Start at the ★.

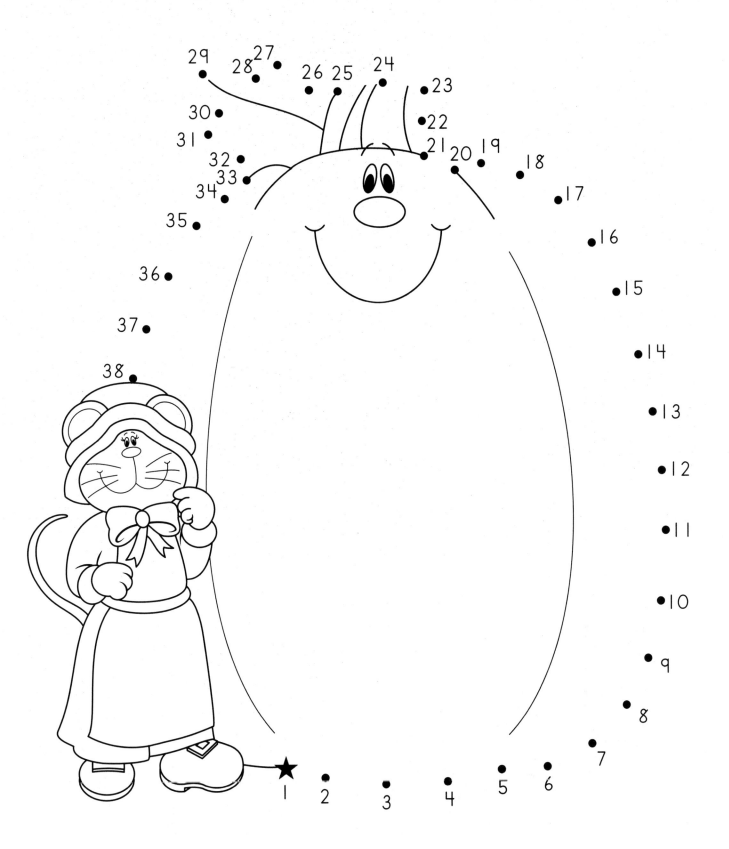

# Gobble up these tasty Thanksgiving snacks!

## Top-It-Yourself Popcorn

Enjoy popcorn with a twist. Have an adult help you make a batch of plain popcorn. Divide the popcorn into several bowls. Cover each bowl of popcorn with a different topping. Toppings could include brown sugar and cinnamon, Parmesan cheese, seasoned salt, honey, melted cheddar cheese, chocolate syrup, or butterscotch syrup. Make sure to have an adult help you melt any hot toppings. See which kind of popcorn is your favorite.

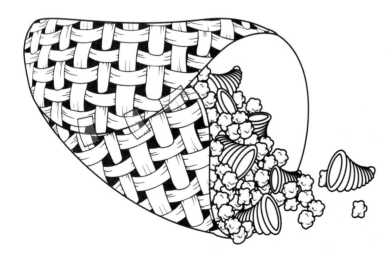

## Cornucopia Snacks

Make a snack mix to put in the cornucopia craft on the next page. Combine cone-shaped corn snacks and crunchy cereal in a big bowl. Scoop up the snack mix with your cornucopia craft. Share the snack mix with friends.

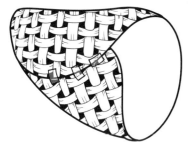

**Completed Cornucopia**

# Make your own cornucopia.

1. Color the cornucopia pattern with harvest colors, then carefully cut it out.

2. Roll the pattern into a cone shape, leaving one end open. Tape the edges together.

# Color by number to discover a colorful harvest food.

1 = yellow    2 = red    3 = brown    4 = green    5 = black    6 = blue

# Gather a group of friends and play these fun games.

## Thanksgiving Feast Tag

Choose one person to be "It." If "It" tags another player, then that player becomes "It." Players are safe from being tagged if they stop running before "It" catches them and then name a food they like to eat during Thanksgiving. Players remain safe until they move again.

## Hot Potato

Choose one person to start and stop the music. Have everyone else sit in a circle. Pass a potato around the circle to the music. Pretend the potato is very hot. When the music stops, the person caught holding the potato is out. Start the music again and continue. The winner is the last remaining player in the circle.

# Use the secret code below to answer the questions.

What were some foods eaten at the first Thanksgiving?

What were some foods not eaten at the first Thanksgiving?

What kind of key does not open a door?

Find and circle 10 foods or drinks that were not present at the first Thanksgiving feast.

# Circle the two cornucopias that are the same. Color.

# How many words can you make from the letters in this word?
## HARVEST

1. _____
2. _____
3. _____
4. _____
5. _____
6. _____
7. _____
8. _____
9. _____
10. _____
11. _____
12. _____
13. _____
14. _____
15. _____
16. _____

17. _____
18. _____
19. _____
20. _____
21. _____
22. _____
23. _____
24. _____
25. _____
26. _____
27. _____
28. _____
29. _____
30. _____

# Follow the directions to make a turkey centerpiece.

1. Color and cut out the turkey patterns and stand.
2. Tape the ends of the turkey stand together to form a ring.
3. Glue the turkey feathers to the turkey body.
4. Glue the turkey to the stand and place it on the dinner table.

Completed Turkey

# Help the mouse find his way to the cheese.

# Follow the directions to make these corn crafts.

## Corncob Painting

1. Gather several dried corncobs, some with the kernels still intact and some without.
2. Fill several trays with different colors of tempera paint.
3. Roll a corncob in a tray of paint.
4. Roll the corncob on a piece of construction paper, then allow the paint to dry.
5. Repeat with different corncobs and different colors of paint to create new designs.

## Harvest Corn

1. Cover a short cardboard tube with glue.
2. Roll the cardboard tube in a tray of colored popcorn kernels until the tube is covered.
3. Allow the glue to dry.
4. Glue some raffia to the inside of one end of the tube to look like corn silk.

Connect the dots to find a yummy Thanksgiving food. Start at the ★.

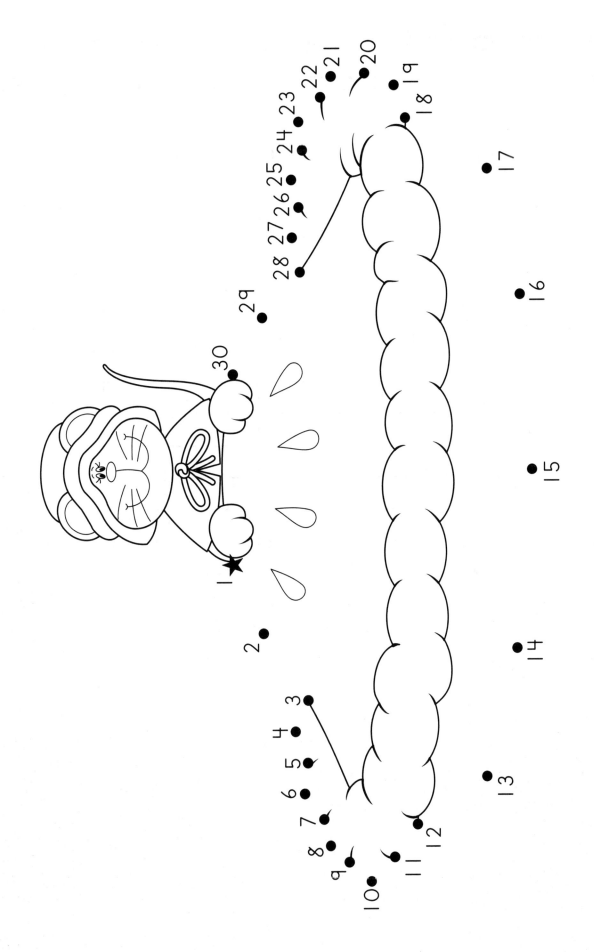

Use the word list to make your own word search in the grid. Then, see if a friend can find all the words.

Word List

| | | | |
|---|---|---|---|
| CABIN | MAST | SAIL | TRUNK |
| CAPTAIN | OCEAN | SEA | VOYAGE |
| DECK | PILGRIMS | SHIP | WAVES |

Color the picture of Squanto teaching the Pilgrim to fertilize.

# Use the word list to complete the crossword puzzle.

**Word List**

COOK
FEATHERS
FISH
GOBBLE
PIE
SHIP
TURKEY

## Across

2. Turkeys, like other birds, are covered with these.
6. This food, eaten at the first Thanksgiving, comes from oceans, lakes, and streams.
7. A word meaning "to prepare food" or "a person who prepares food" is _____.

## Down

1. A dessert made from apples, pecans, or pumpkins in a pastry crust is a _____.
3. This meat is eaten with stuffing or cranberry sauce.
4. *Mayflower* was the name of the Pilgrims' _____.
5. A turkey makes this sound.

# Find and circle the words from the word list below.

S M D G W F K O J A H L M
N V A E N R I N Q X P U I
F H A Y S T A C K E Y M G
H C V T H A N K F U L T N
B F O M F A M I L Y S E M
E R H R E X L Y K A T P L
N I A P N A M Z E A S U T
J E R L U U L F R P Q M L
Y N V E Y R C B B K U P O
M D E N M Q E O V K A K E
V S S T V L N W P I S I
P T Y E R Q U H I H N
Z B C G A T H E R A G

## Word List

CELEBRATE          FRIENDS          PLENTY
CORNUCOPIA         GATHER           PUMPKIN
FAMILY             HARVEST          SQUASH
FEAST              HAYSTACK         THANKFUL
                   MEAL

Find and circle 11 things wrong with this Thanksgiving picture.

# Make these napkins rings to use at Thanksgiving dinner.

1. Color the napkin rings and cut them out.
2. Tape the ends of each pattern together at the dashed line, forming a ring.
3. Slide each napkin ring over a dinner napkin. Place the napkins and napkin rings on the table.

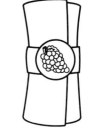

Completed Napkin Ring

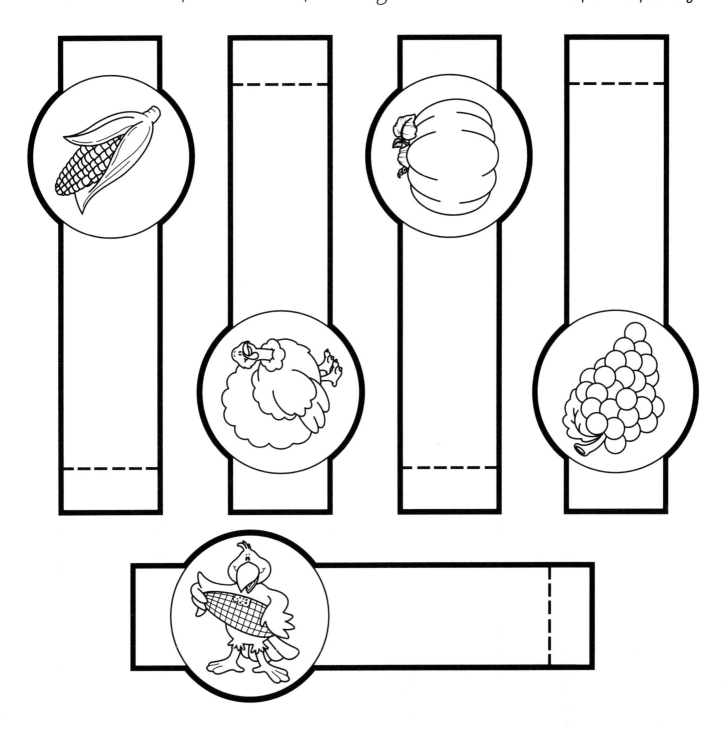

# Gather friends and play Pin the Wattle on the Turkey.

1. Color and cut out the turkey and wattles.
2. Attach the turkey to a wall.
3. Put a piece of tape on the back of each wattle.
4. Spin each child around ten times and have him try to pin the wattle on the turkey's beak.